Ghosts

of the

Old Jail

Ghosts of the Old Jail

Frances A. R. Allshouse

Director of the Old Jail Museum

&

Andrew B. Allshouse

Coauthor and illustrator

FIRST EDITION

133.129 - dc22

ISBN: 1492918466

ISBN-13: 978-1492918462

To the souls of the Old Jail . . .

The lost ones spending eternity there

and the hearty ones striving to keep history alive.

Truly, the Old Jail would be a cold and empty place without you.

Ghosts of the Old Jail

CONTENTS

Contents

FOREWORD

It's almost impossible to work at the Old Jail Museum for any length of time and not have something unexplainable happen. The paranormal is nearly a fact of daily life rather than an unusual occurrence. It's something you get used to, like a squeaky stair or a ticking clock.

Over the years, the staff of the Old Jail Museum have amassed an impressive collection of strange and eerie stories, and, of course, these are the tales most often requested by visitors. This book is an effort to collect and retell the museum's oddest and spookiest stories.

We hope you enjoy.

-The Staff of the Old Jail Museum

Ghosts of the Old Jail

PREFACE

As the Museum Director I hope that you find this trip through the strange and macabre history and happenings of the Old Jail illuminating. The veil between "reality" and the "supernatural" is thinner than most realize and while I can't guarantee the legitimacy of each incident conveyed in this book, I can say that the vast majority of the stories were told to me as first or second-hand occurrences by ladies and gentlemen whose statements I have no reason to doubt. As for my own experiences, I know that there is more than meets the eye within the walls of these buildings.

So after years of requests for a compilation of the ghostlier history of the Museum, this is my attempt to pull back the veil.

-*Frances Allshouse*

Preface

INTRODUCTION: A BRIEF HISTORY

Before we delve into the jail's hauntings, it's important to understand a bit of its history.

The Old Fauquier County Jail complex was built in two parts. The front, or brick, portion of the jail was built in 1808 and originally included four cells, each of which is said to have been approved to house 40 prisoners. The jailor came by periodically, but in the interim, convicts broke windows, fought, attempted to escape and worse. As you can imagine, conditions for the prisoners were poor to say the least. In 1818, the Commonwealth of Virginia actually sued the jailor for the prison's filthy condition.

In 1823, after only 15 years of use, the brick jail was deemed insufficient and a new stone jail was built just to the rear of the older structure. The 1808 jail was then converted into a house for the jailor. A kitchen made of the leftover stones from the "new jail" was added in 1824. Incidentally, in the same year, the town installed a set of stocks, a whipping post and a pillory in the yard just in front of the jailor's home. It is, as yet, unclear when this form of punishment ceased in Warrenton.

    The 1823 stone jail, like its predecessor, had four cells, but it also had stoves in each cell to provide the prisoners with warmth and an exercise yard. From the late 1870's until the 1890's the exercise yard was also used as a hanging yard and a three-man gallows is said to have stood there.

    Despite numerous calls for a new prison to be built, the stone jail remained in use for the next 143 years. Consider that for a moment. When constructed, Thomas Jefferson was still alive and the United States was only 47 years old. Over the following century and a half, it was used as a prison during the Civil War, reconstruction, the suffrage movement, prohibition, two world wars and the civil rights movement just to name a few.

    In 1964, plans were underway to build a new jail for Fauquier County and the old jail's 1808 and 1823 structures were slated for demolition. Through the combined efforts of numerous community activists, the Fauquier Historical Society was founded with the purpose of preserving and maintaining the old jail complex as a museum.

Today, the Old Jail is a museum focusing on the history of Fauquier County. The artifacts that make up the museum's exhibitions have all been donated by generous local citizens.

A Brief History

Map of the Old Jail

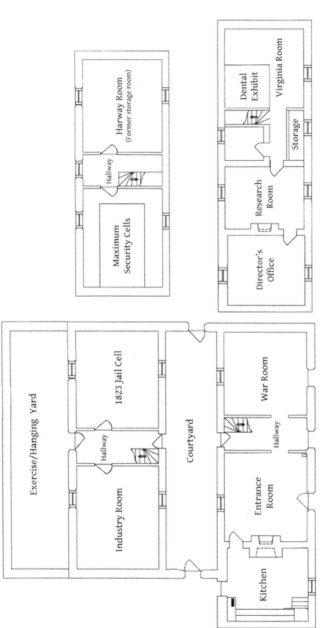

Second Floor

Harway Room (former storage room)

Hallway

Maximum Security Cells

Virginia Room

Dental Exhibit

Storage

Research Room

Director's Office

First Floor

Exercise/Hanging Yard

1823 Jail Cell

Hallway

Industry Room

Courtyard

War Room

Hallway

Entrance Room

Kitchen

CHILDREN OF THE JAIL

It was a quiet Monday afternoon. Quiet except for one thing. The ghost hunters. They had made their appointment months in advance and finally the day had come for them to investigate the Old Jail Museum. The museum director had met them at the front door, showed them around, told them about the spots where most of the activity had happened, and then left them to their own devises. She listened from her office as they moved from one room to the next - calling out to the spirits and asking for a response.

Generally, these sort of groups found a "sweet spot" quickly and settled in to take their readings, but this group was different. They seemed to be moving through the rooms fast. The director guessed they must not be finding much. Too bad, they seemed genuinely interested in the jail.

Having sped through the rest of the museum, the last room was the kitchen. Directly above the kitchen, the museum director sat in her office updating the artifact catalogue and listening to the ghost hunters. Seemed like they were putting a lot more effort into this room. Maybe they'd found their sweet spot after all. They took pictures, asked and then demanded the spirits talk to them. But still there were no signs that the ghosts were willing to communicate.

They had all but decided to pack up and go home, but one pressed the group to try one more thing. It wasn't anything special, really, just a small rubber ball. But maybe, just maybe, if they were lucky, the young spirits of the jail would like to play.

The ghost hunters placed the ball in the middle of the floor. "If anyone is with us, please move the ball," they implored. And suddenly there was excitement. The ball, it would seem, had moved.

From above the director scoffed. "Of course the ball moved," she muttered to herself distractedly. "The floorboards are warped and there's a slope to the whole room."

Unaware of her thoughts, again and again the team of paranormals retrieved the ball, placed it in the same spot on the floor and watched as it traveled the same course. "Are you playing with us?" asked one of the team leaders at length.

He received no response. But above, the hair on the back of the director's neck was standing on end. A moment after the leader had asked his question, a little girl had giggled in her right ear.

She still doubted that the investigators had had an encounter, but she certainly had.

The Marks That Some Have Left

THE MARKS THAT SOME HAVE LEFT

The earliest records of the 1808 jail show that some female prisoners had little choice but to bring their children with them into the cold, damp, dark and hard living conditions offered by the jail. After the 1808 prison became the jailor's residence, jailors' families lived there too.

A number of these children left their mark on the building in one way or another. On a pane of glass in a second floor window, where once was a child's bedroom, the name Josie is scratched in a child-like scrawl. But not all marks the children left appear to be this simple.

In 1988, during the early years of the museum, a volunteer was working late into the night. A new set of bookshelves and a door sill had been installed that morning and he had opted to stay late to paint them. As he labored away on the bookshelves, he paused for a second thinking that he heard laughter. Looking around, he found no one else was there and all the doors were locked just as he left them. He reasoned that the explanation was simple; this was after all an old building and in its 180 year life it was bound to pick up a few creaks. Besides, it was late and he figured his mind must have been playing tricks on him.

He went back to work but 10 minutes later he stopped again. This time he was sure he had heard something. He would have sworn on any other night that he had heard two sets of footsteps run through the room he was in; but it could not have been as the doors never moved and he knew that he was the only living soul in the building. So, once more he went back to work even more resolute to finish his task that night. As his work drew to an end, he stood back to admire his progress. But something wasn't right.

The Marks That Some Have Left

The freshly painted doorsill had already been marred. How had that happened? He looked closer and there before his shocked eyes was a single tiny footprint...a child's footprint. The intrepid volunteer hurriedly packed. He'd worry about painting over the footprint tomorrow and let the children have the rest of the night to play.

To this day some say that when all is still you can hear little footsteps run through the hall of the old jail. Maybe some of the children are still playing long after their bodies have returned to dust. Then again some might be looking for new playmates.

STRANGE SOUNDS

Many docents and volunteers at the museum have reported hearing sounds in the 1808 jail when they know that they are alone. The most common complaint is that there is someone walking around on the second floor. Those who have experienced the phantom footsteps have said that after hearing the footsteps above they go on about their business supposing that the museum director has gotten to work early and is busy pursuing a particular project. At length, part of the opening routine will lead the volunteer upstairs where they bid the director good morning only to find that the director isn't there. Nor is anyone else.

Rarer than the footfalls, is the dragging sound that some of the museum's volunteers have experienced. The setting is the same, a volunteer or docent enters the museum early in the morning assuming that they are the first to arrive. Shortly after their arrival, the grating sound of a heavy object being dragged across the floor above echoes through the old building. Once more the docent assumes that the director is moving items, but finds upon inspection that they are alone.

Another strange sound is "the whistler". This spirit makes its presence known by producing three whistled notes as if to say hello. The three tones are always the same and always clear. Sometimes the whistler repeats its trio of notes, sometimes not. Sometimes the whistler sounds close at hand as if you might turn and find someone standing right beside you, and at other times it sounds so very lost and far away.

While many of the sounds heard in the museum can be linked to a particular area, the whistler can be heard throughout the buildings. The three shrill notes have been heard early in the morning and late at night, in the maximum security cell and from the other side of a barred window. But in all cases the listener is alone.

It would seem that the whistler is repeating the song of a past resident of the jail, the question is was it a voluntary resident or one that was incarcerated.

MAKING AN EXAMPLE OF THOMAS JEWITT

During the Civil War, countless scenes of horror played out in the streets of Warrenton, but none were more chilling than the tale of Thomas Jewitt.

Jewitt was a young captain connected with a Maine regiment. In the summer of 1862, he was accused of desertion to the enemy and was remanded to the Warrenton jail. Tried and found guilty, he was sentenced to be executed. But the sentence went beyond just Jewitt's fate. His entire division was also ordered to witness the execution.

At half past eleven on the morning of August 14, Jewitt was taken from the jail. He was loaded into a four-horse wagon and was ordered to be seated on his own coffin. His only companion was his regimental chaplain. Driven a short distance from the Jail, Jewitt was met with the sight of the three brigades of his regiment forming three sides of a square.

They were on an elevated piece of ground from which the execution could be seen in every direction. The wagon entered the hollow square and drove all around the periphery so that each man could clearly see the condemned. The wagon came to a stop and Jewitt was led out, the coffin unloaded onto the ground and Jewitt ordered to be seated atop it again. The chaplain spoke a few quiet words, offered a prayer, shook Jewitt's hand and walked away.

A few feet away, ten muskets lay stacked on the ground. Eight were loaded with powder and shot, two had only blanks. Ten men from his regiment were called forward and ordered to pick up a musket, none knowing if the weapon he held would be deadly or not.

"Ready, Aim, Fire!" came the order and the report of ten muskets rent the air. Across the hollow square, the force of the shots lifted Jewitt from his place on the coffin and threw him to the ground.

As the regiments filed past his body, the message was clear . . . this was the fate of all traitors.

MISCELLANEOUS HALLWAY HAPPENINGS

The second floor hallway of the 1823 jail has been the site of several eerie incidents. Workers and visitors in the museum have often felt the urge to close the door that faces the maximum security cell. Why? It seems that many are gripped by the sense that someone or something is watching them from the darkened doorway of the opposing cell. A glance over the shoulder confirms that they are alone, but for some, the feeling cannot be shaken and they are compelled to close the door to block the unseen prying eyes.

Those who have experienced this may well not be alone. Small, rapidly moving shadows have been seen scuttling about in the area. A paranormal investigator reported seeing a human-sized shadow run from the cell on the right through the hall and into maximum security. A loud popping sound like metal striking metal was heard immediately after.

An intern working to install a display in the second floor hall reported a strange interaction with a group of visitors. It was a family with a young boy. She greeted the group and they went on their way reading the signs in the display rooms. Moments later, the child ran back to the hallway and asked, "What are you doing?" The intern began to explain her work, but the child cut her off. "Not you! Him!" He pointed to a corner of the hallway that appeared to the intern to be empty. Yet the child persisted, staring into the corner and asking questions. At length he seemed satisfied and darted into the next room.

WORKING LATE

Despite the jail's dark past, most who work in the buildings report feeling safe and comfortable. Most feel welcome, but one was urged to leave.

In 2007, the museum had been undergoing various repairs. Chief among these was a complete repainting of the 1808 jail. Repainting had meant that every artifact had had to be carefully wrapped, boxed up and stored in another area of the museum. After weeks of work, the display cabinets were finally restored to their original places and the long task of refilling them could begin. There was just one problem. Weeks before, a local boy scout troop had arranged for a tour of the museum. Thinking the repairs would be completed well before the tour date, museum staff had agreed. But the work had taken a bit longer than expected, and the result was that one room, the War Room, remained without its artifacts and the scouts would be there tomorrow.

There was but one solution, someone would need to stay late and finish the room. One worker agreed.

She had stayed late many times before for various programs or to finish one project or other. She knew where the artifacts were stored and the order in which they needed to go back into the cases.

It was nothing, really, should be no problem at all. If she was lucky, she figured she'd be home before midnight. The last rays of daylight faded away as she retrieved the first set of boxes from their storage place in the 1823 jail. Those boxes went quickly and soon she needed to retrieve another set.

As she entered the old stone jail this time, the feeling in the building had changed dramatically. It was eerie and claustrophobic and she kept feeling as though the big steel doors were about to be slammed and locked behind her. Of course, that didn't make any sense and she knew it. The huge skeleton keys needed to lock the doors were safely tucked away in her back pocket. She shrugged off the unsettling feeling. Surely, her imagination was getting the better of her. It was an old jail with a history of violence and hauntings . . . of course it was a little creepy at night when she knew she was alone. So with that, she collected a few more boxes and returned to the task at hand.

When those boxes had been emptied and she returned for more she realized that not only had the uneasy feeling not gone away, it had grown stronger . . . a lot stronger. She simply didn't want to enter the jail at all now. But she thought it was silly not to, so she strode in and picked up the next stack. She wouldn't allow the scouts to be disappointed by unfinished displays just because she was getting anxious. Besides, there were just a couple big boxes left. If she made two more trips right now, she wouldn't have to go back again later. To her, that seemed like a good idea.

She put her boxes down in the alley, steeled her nerves and turned again to face the century-old steel doors. But this time she could barely force herself to enter the 1823 jail and the farther she went the more she wanted to leave.   Standing in the 1823 cell and picking up the second to last box, a single thought suddenly pierced her mind as if it had come from someone else "You do not belong here." And a moment later, "*Get out!*"

She didn't need to be told again. If someone truly didn't want her there, she had no business invading their space.

She took her box and locked the door behind her realizing too late that she hadn't turned off the lights, but knowing that no force could compel her to reenter the building that night.

Arriving early the next morning just as the sky began to lighten, she unlocked the building she had half fled the night before only to find the atmosphere calm and peaceful. The final box was retrieved without incident and the display made ready just in time to greet the scouts.

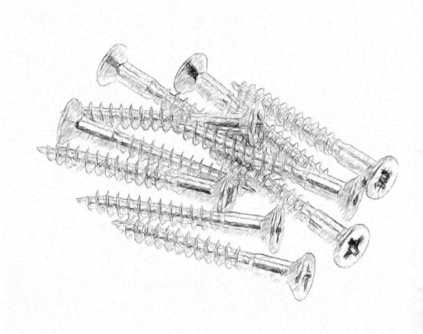

TWENTY FOUR

Late one summer a member of the museum staff was working with an intern on a project. The student had chosen to research the history of the jail's exercise yard and develop and present a display in the yard. The intern had thoroughly researched her topic, finding information regarding everything from bathroom facilities that had been available in the yard to the executions that had occurred there.

The day had finally come for her to install the display, all she needed were a few screws to secure the top on her piece. Museum staff searched their supplies finding that there were two boxes available. One box contained exactly 24 screws; the precise number that the intern needed. A staff member brought the box to the intern and began helping install the display. The first two pieces went together easily, so they started work on the third.

She went to the box to pick up some more screws. But something didn't look right. There

Ghosts of the Old Jail

should be twelve screws left, but what remained in the box looked like less than twelve. She counted them. Eight. That was odd, she had counted them herself. There had definitely been 24. She counted again. Still eight.

Neither she nor the intern had dropped any and neither of them were holding any extra screws. Where did they go? Oh well, it didn't really matter she supposed as they still had a few more in the other box. So, she left the intern to go retrieve the rest of the needed supplies. Returning a few moments later with four screws in hand, she glanced in the box once more. But now there seemed to be more than before. She counted again and came up with twelve. The intern hadn't added any and the ones that she had picked up were still tucked safely in her hand. The two laughed – someone obviously had a sense of humor.

THE MYSTERIOUS WOMAN

One of the most vivid sightings in the Old Jail occurred in the winter of 1994. A contractor who had been working to restore various areas in the jail complex arrived early one cold, February morning. Typically, he would have been accompanied by his son, but icy weather had made some roads too treacherously slick to pass. So today the contractor was alone as he set about preparing for the day ahead of him.

He had begun to scrape the stairwell in the 1823 jail the day before, and now it was waiting for him to finish it. If the day went well he might be ready to begin painting tomorrow. He gathered his tools and materials and carried them to the top of the steep steel stairs where they would be close at hand as he needed them. He settled himself in, half sitting and half standing, about mid-way down the stairs. It was obvious that the paint hadn't been touched in the last twenty years. It was in terrible condition and he knew that this section would take a good deal of time to prepare for repainting.

As he began scraping the flaking paint from the wall, he was suddenly aware that he was not alone. Just inches to his right a figure had appeared standing at the top of the stairs. Backing quickly down the flight toward the door, he took in the sight that had appeared before him. The figure was that of a small, slender woman. She wore a floor-length, lacy, blue dress and her yellow-blonde hair was gathered to the side and bound with a white ribbon. She remained perfectly silent and stood eerily still for several seconds before fading away as suddenly as she had materialized.

The worker was stunned by what he had just witnessed, but at length he managed to regain his composure and return to work. But the phantom had left such an impression on him that he felt compelled to share his story.

In a report that he prepared for the museum, he spoke in detail of his experience and summarized it by saying, "I am convinced that I have met a ghost!"

The Mysterious Woman

INDIAN-GERMAN-EXECUTION

It was a typical day in the museum, visitors came, toured and went on their way at a steady pace. But it was about to become very odd indeed. A young man stepped through the door. In his hand he held a small electronic box. He stared at it intently, watching the lights swirl about on its screen. The docent on duty gave him the usual introduction to the buildings and he proceeded on his way through the museum.

As he wandered around the room, an electronic voice suddenly rang out. "Indian!" it declared as he stood before the Native American exhibit. He continued on; reading the signs in the display cabinets and keeping an eye trained on the box. As he neared the World War Two collection, the little box called out, "German!" And, sure enough, on the other side of the glass sat a WWII German officer's uniform. Making his way through the 1823 jail, he finished his tour at the exercise, or hanging yard. "Execution!" sang the box.

When the young man reached the door, the docent puzzled over the box he'd watched so carefully. He must have understood the questions that were forming in her mind. It was a ghost meter, he explained. The newest thing in ghost hunting technology. It picked up on the electromagnetic energy in a room and, if there was enough, it would say something. Effectively allowing the deceased to communicate with the living.

It is unknown if the energy in the rooms set off the ghost meter or if it was the artifacts themselves. Or maybe it was a resident spirit who'd heard the tour enough times to give it himself. No matter the source, on that day the ghost meter had enabled one visitor to have his own personal tour!

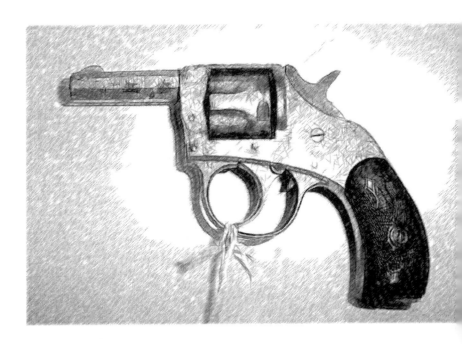

Willie Davis Doesn't Like That

WILLIE DAVIS DOESN'T LIKE THAT

Willie Davis shot and killed Southern Railway detective John Holcomb Woodson on Monday, August 5, 1946. Davis escaped arrest and eluded capture until August 7 when he held the Musselman family of Catlett at gunpoint while he attempted to steal their food and money. The Musselmans managed to subdue the criminal and he was brought to the Fauquier County jail where he was held during his trial. Davis was convicted of murder in the first degree and was sentenced to be electrocuted. His sentence was carried out at the State Penitentiary on July 18, 1947.

Sixty years later, the museum director asked her interns to prepare a new exhibition. The display would be housed in the 1823 jail's maximum security cell and would tell the stories of several well-known Fauquier criminals who had spent time in the jail complex. Among the criminals named would be the infamous Willie Davis.

The interns were thorough in their research and when they had completed their task they had produced an excellent set of prisoner stories among which Davis' was surely the most impressive. Not only was there an account of his crime, but there were three photos: one showed the weapon he'd used to kill John Woodson, another the Mussleman family and a final image depicted the man himself. With everything in order, all that was left was to hang the accounts where visitors could read them. Carefully mounting the pieces and affixing them to the walls with heavy duty double-faced foam tape, the director figured the display should last a few years before normal wear demanded it be replaced.

Entering the maximum security cell the following morning, the director was surprised to find Willie Davis' story, his photo and the picture of his murder weapon on the floor. She sighed as she picked up the pieces. Sometimes signs just didn't adhere well to these walls. After all, the paint here was flaking a bit. At least all the other signs, including the image of the Musselmans, remained firmly attached to the walls.

She remounted the Davis story and images and set about her other responsibilities, but again, come morning, she found everything related to the case, save the Musselman family portrait, lying on the floor.

Over the next several months, replacing the Davis signs became a weekly task. Though they were re-cut, remounted, new tape found to attach them to the walls and different spots selected for the story to be featured, each time, the story and all but the picture of the Musselman family were found crumpled on the floor.

At length, the director had come up with a new way of displaying the stories and it was time to replace all of the signs. She'd put the Davis story on the other side of the room this time. It would have copies of the original newspaper clippings that detailed the case. And it would be affixed to smooth metal duct work rather than the porous wall. Within weeks, the story began peeling from its backing, curling away as if to escape. Soon it too was found face down on the floor. Is it all coincidence? Or does Willie Davis just not want his story told?

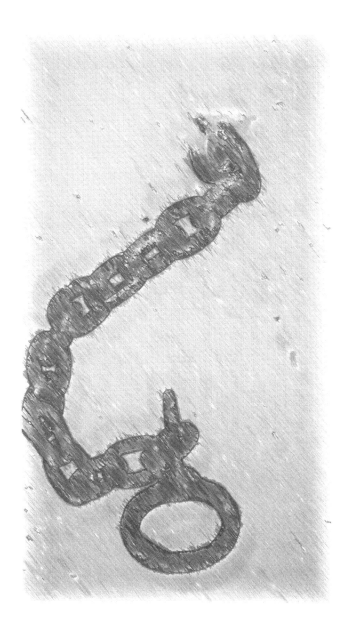

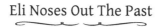

ELI NOSES OUT THE PAST

It's a little-known fact that the Old Jail
Museum has an open door policy when it comes to
pets. Animals are welcome, so long as they are well-
behaved.

In 2010, a visitor brought a dog with her into
the museum. His name was Eli and, unbeknownst to
the docent, he was in training to be something great.
It was good to bring Eli out to public places since he'd
be working with the public for the rest of his life, but
today he was acting very strangely. When he and his
mistress entered the museum's kitchen, the normally
laid-back dog became a flurry of energy. He kept
tapping his paw on the iron hearth and looking at his
mistress. She recognized that behavior, but in a place
like this, it didn't make any sense. Moreover, Eli
repeatedly made his way to the stairs leading to the
bedroom above and tapped his paw on them all the
while staring at his mistress.

Despite looking elsewhere in the museum, Eli kept pulling his mistress back to the kitchen. Confused by Eli's behavior, the visitor asked the docent on duty if she might bring another dog in. This one was highly trained. He was "Mr. No-nonsense" in every way.

She brought her veteran in and led him around the museum. When they entered the kitchen, to her surprise, he became very interested in the bedroom stairs. But being unable to gain access to them continued to search the room. When he came to the hearth, he immediately laid down, his paws outstretched toward the iron hearth.

Now that was very strange. The docent on duty who had been watching all of this unfold, finally asked, "Are the dogs trying to tell you something?" The visitor answered with a question of her own, "Has anything unusual ever happened in the kitchen?" "What do you mean by 'unusual'?" asked the docent. "Well, have you ever heard of a cadaver dog?" Both Eli and Mr. No-nonsense had given her clear signals. Someone had died in this kitchen. The docent was amazed. Museum staff didn't usually tell visitors about it, but there was a story that the wife of one of the jailors had died of burns she received when her skirts caught fire at the hearth. Over one hundred years later and somehow the cadaver dogs had known.

THE LADY IN WHITE

In the late 1800's, the wife of one of the jailors was busy preparing a meal for the prisoners. You see, as wife to the jailor, she was paid a salary independent from that of her husband so that she could feed the inmates. This was not a large salary mind you, and the wife of the jailor had to work hard to make cheap food palatable even for the prisoners.

As she hurried in her work, tending the open-hearth fire and positioning the bubbling pots so that they would receive the perfect amount of heat, her long skirts swished across the kitchen's uneven floorboards. She leaned close to the hearth inspecting the contents of her pots and pans and silently the hem of her skirt fell into the coals. All too quickly, flames engulfed her. Taken aback by the shock of it all, she could do little to put out the flames until it as too late and soon she had been horribly burned. She died shortly thereafter.

A century later, early one morning the Old Jail's board of directors convened in the entrance room. The assembled members were seated and had just begun their meeting when a woman in a gleaming white dress emerged from the kitchen. Everyone stopped what they were doing, some of them mid-sentence. They were all transfixed by this gleaming figure. She was unknown to anyone and paid the gathering no heed as she turned in front of them, passed through a display case, and walked silently through the wall to the right of the door.

The board of directors dropped everything and without a word, the meeting was adjourned.

It was not until sometime later that the story of the jailor's wife was uncovered and the lady in white was identified.

More than a decade has passed since the lady in white made her spectacular exit at the board meeting. Perhaps she'll make another appearance in due time.

Ghosts of the Old Jail

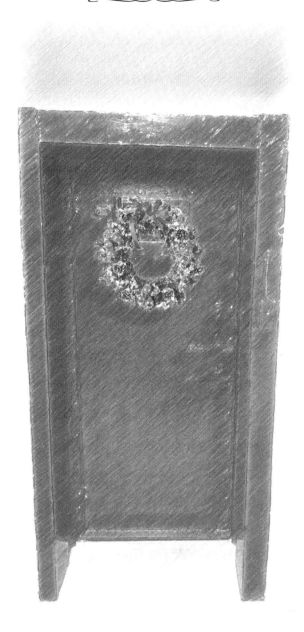

A CHRISTMAS VISIT

Christmas is one of those few days each year when the museum closes, but on one particular Christmas day in the mid 1990's the museum was in fact open. It seemed that there was a group from Europe coming for a short visit to Virginia. They'd only be in the area the one day. Could they possibly arrange for a tour of the Old Jail Museum? The visit had been okayed and now, several weeks later, a docent sat waiting for her Yule time guests.

She glanced at the clock before going back to her book – they would be here any moment now. As she waited quietly, the stillness of the building was rent by a sharp click. It was a distinctly familiar sound to those who worked at the jail. That was the sound of the thumb latch being opened on the door in the kitchen. These days the door opened upon a small landing that staff used to store the trashcan, brooms and the like, but years ago a steep set of stairs leading to the small bedroom above lay beyond the door.

Once heard, there was no mistaking that latch for any other sound. Yet it was utterly impossible that it would have opened. She was alone and that latch took some effort to open. Rising from her seat, the docent found that the door was closed, the latch seemingly untouched – but movement from above caught her eye. Glancing up, she saw that the heavy iron chandelier above was swinging wildly. No draft was strong enough to move that chandelier.

MR. Mc G

The tale of Mr. McGracken (everyone calls him Mc G) is one of the Jail's oldest and best-known ghost stories. Mc G came to the jail in the early 1920's after burning down his own home. It would seem that he was convinced his family was conspiring against him to seize his home. So, he decided that the best way to prevent this from happening was to set fire to his house and in so doing commit suicide. Despite his plans, the old man was rescued from the burning building and delivered to the old jail. He was charged with attempted suicide and arson. Upon arrival he was in a terrible state, his long white beard darkened by smoke, his hair unwashed and streaked with soot and grease. Not long after he was imprisoned, Mc G contracted pneumonia and died in the second floor holding cell of the 1823 prison.

But, of course, that is not the end of his tale. Months passed and Mr. Mc G had been all but forgotten when a young woman was arrested for a misdemeanor and was placed in the same cell where Mc G had taken his last breath months before. During her trial, the judge asked the young woman how she had been treated while incarcerated. Her treatment had been fair, she replied, but she did have one complaint. It seemed that while in prison she received no visitors during the day, but each night the same man returned to her cell; a little old man with a long, charcoal-stained white beard and greasy unwashed hair; and each night he tried to steal her blankets. The judge questioned the young lady about this man and she descried in detail Mr. Mc G's appearance despite never hearing of or seeing Mc G before.

Since the jail was opened as a museum, numerous visitors have seen the mournful figure of a man on the second floor of the jail. His description is always the same: small man, greasy hair, long soot-stained white beard.

If you ever see Mr. Mc G, do tell him to keep warm.

Mirrored Apparition

MIRRORED APPARITION

It had been a slow day on February 3rd, 2012. Of course, February was normally a slow month at the museum. Post Christmas rush, but before the spring warm-up, the docent on duty wasn't expecting to greet many visitors. So, he was pleasantly surprised when a large group made its way through the door. Rising from his seat, he gave the group a short history of the buildings before sending them on their way to explore.

As the group moved along, someone approached with a question. When the visitor's question had been answered, she left the room and the docent glanced at the mirror in front of which they had been standing. He'd thought he was alone in

 the room, but obviously he was wrong, because there, reflected in the mirror, he clearly

saw a woman standing next to him.

Another question, he thought, as he turned to address the lady. But there was no one there. How had she come and gone so quickly? He looked into the mirror again, and there she stood right next to him. She wore a long, drab, muddy-colored dress and had dark, shoulder-length hair.

He stared at her for a time, trying to wrap his mind around what he was seeing – and as he stared she began to slowly fade away. Vaporizing before his eyes and finally disappearing. This day had been more exciting than the docent ever thought it was going to be.

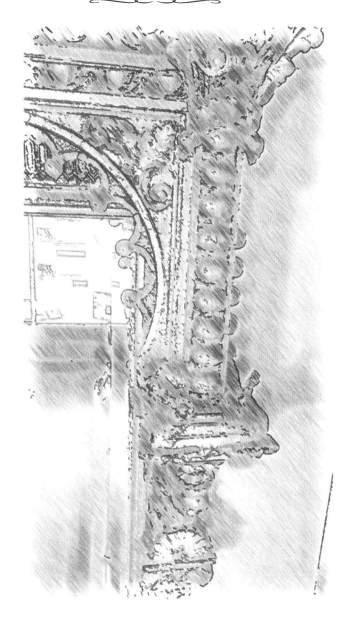

A GRUESOME SPECTACLE

Beginning in the 1870's, several men suffered the same slow, strangulating death on a three-man gallows that lay within the jail's exercise yard. The names of most of these men have been lost to time, but one of the stories has survived. The story of John Williams and Winter Payne haunts people even today. Each man had been accused of committing horrifying and unspeakable murders, each man had been convicted and sentenced to death, and each day that passed since their arrest brought a greater sense of anger and unrest from the people of Warrenton. They were anxious to see these men hang for the lives they had so ruthlessly snuffed out. As dawn broke on the morning of July 11, 1879, the bloodlust of the townspeople reached its breaking point as hordes attempted to force their way into the jail to witness Williams' and Payne's morning executions. Most of the crowd was denied its gruesome spectacle . . . only small children who had climbed a tree that stood on the outside of the yard saw what happened next.

Both men were led to the gallows from their cells, both men caused the wood to groan under their feet, both men had the coarse rope tightened around their necks, both men waited for the executioner to make his final move, both men met their fate, and both bodies were slowly lowered from the crude wooden structure.

Waiting at the small side door was John Williams' family who sobbingly collected his body, but no one waited for Winter Payne. He was taken to a nearby field and buried in an unmarked grave. Don't believe me? The full story was published in the New York Times on July 12, 1879, with more gruesome details than I have the stomach to relate.

Disquiet in the Library

The summer of 2011 was proving to be a busy one and, as it was the weekend, on this day there were even more visitors than usual. As the docent greeted guests and attended to her duties, suddenly from above there was a loud crash. It sounded like a large pile of books had just come hurtling off a desk smashing to the floor in the museum's research room. Maybe one of those stacks of books the director had been cataloging had toppled. The docent made her way upstairs and opened the research room door expecting to find a heap of books strewn across the floor, but to her surprise, nothing seemed out of place.

Returning to her spot, downstairs just in time to meet another wave of visitors, it wasn't long before she began hearing loud, stomping footfalls tracking between the research room and the director's office. Some might have dashed back up the steps, but she knew there was no one in the research room and she knew the director's office was locked. She wouldn't find anyone there.

Time passed and amid the stomping another crash was heard in the rooms above. Phantom footsteps might be common, but crashes were cause for concern. Again she checked, and again everything was in its usual place.

For two days, the stomping continued punctuated occasionally by the sound of heavy objects slamming to the floor. A visitor unlucky enough to enter just as a particularly loud crash echoed through the museum asked what was causing all the commotion. "Someone doesn't sound happy," was the only explanation offered.

By 8am Sunday morning, all was quiet and a thorough search of the rooms showed nothing out of place.

Disquiet in the Library

A Breath on His Neck

Of the four young men who walked through the door, on one spring afternoon in 2009, two had visited before and two were out-of-towners. The veteran visitors guided their guests through the front building telling them about some of the interesting things they'd learned during their previous trip.

When they had finished looking through the 1808 jail, the young men's guests asked if there was anything else to see. Oh yes, the men explained there was a whole other building, but they weren't going back out there again. If the guests wanted to see it, fine, but they were on their own.

Thinking their friends were acting rather foolishly, the pair continued into the 1823 jail. They took pictures, and poked some fun at their buddies as they looked about enjoying a thoroughly uneventful visit. This wasn't so bad. What was the big deal? Why had they acted like such wimps?

As the pair proceeded upstairs, they parted ways – one making his way into maximum security while the other remained in the hall taking a few more photos.

The young man in the hallway surveyed the space. He still couldn't see why the others wouldn't come out here. He turned his back to maximum security and raised his camera – and in that moment a warm breath blew across the back of his neck. He whirled around yelling, "Stop it!" at the friend he expected to find standing behind him. But there was no one there. "What!?" came the response from maximum security, followed by hurried footsteps as his comrade emerged from the room. That was strange. He dismissed the event and calmed his friend. It must have been a breeze. This place was sure to be a little drafty.

Remembering that he still hadn't gotten that picture, he tried again to focus his camera. But there it was again – a warm, moist breath on his neck. He turned around more slowly this time, hoping, but not expecting to find his friend standing there. Once again he was alone. "I'm leaving," he declared as he made his way back down the stairs and out the door, leaving his friend behind and hurrying to rejoin the two who wouldn't come with them.

Now he understood, not only was the place haunted, but the ghosts liked to play pranks.

Ghosts of the Old Jail

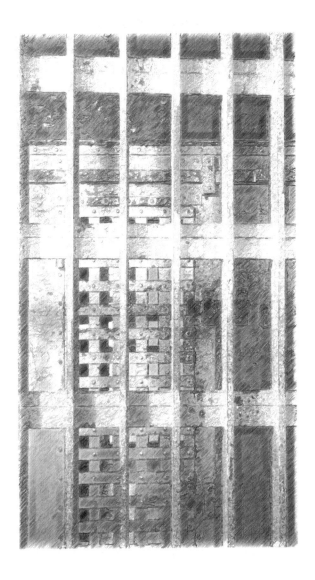

THE GUIDING HAND

It's interesting to note that while the spirits of the second floor of the 1823 jail seem to like to play tricks on men, they sometimes show a protective side to women.

Summers often bring out-of-town visitors to the Old Jail and this afternoon in August 2011 was no different as two English women were making their way through the exhibition rooms. They had just about finished their tour, only the two rooms on the second floor of the 1823 jail remained to be explored.

As they reached the second story, the pair split up – one moving into maximum security while the other looked at the displays in the hall. The woman who had gone into the maximum security cell wasn't there long before she rejoined her friend urging her to go take a look at the cage. As the second read the stories about the prisoners in the maximum security cage, she felt a hand cup her elbow and another touch her back. Briskly, she was led out the door and into the hallway. She turned to her friend to ask why she had led her out of the space, but found that she was standing alone. Glancing across to the opposite room, there stood her companion. Unshaken, she laughed to herself and told her friend what had just happened.

But as it turned out, she had experienced the same thing. As they descended the stairs they chatted about their experience. It was the sort of thing that happened to them all the time in England, but they hadn't expected it here. At the bottom of the stairs stood two other women who had been on the second floor earlier and were now overhearing the conversation.

They were relieved, they said, that it had happened to someone else. They had hesitated saying anything, figuring others would think they were crazy, but they too had been led out of the maximum security cell block by unseen hands. On the same day, the docent on duty reported that two other female visitors also reported being touched when they visited the maximum security cell.

The Guiding Hand

TOUCH

    Volunteers play a huge role at the Old Jail.
They greet guests, organize and index the archives.
They even help maintain and catalog the museum's
artifacts. It was during a cataloging session that one
summer volunteer had an encounter she would never
forget.

    It had been something of a long day. She'd
worked in the office for most of the day inputting
page after page of measurements and descriptions of
artifacts into the museum's catalog database. Finally,
she decided to stretch her legs a bit and go take a few
pictures. After all, photos were meant to go along
with each entry in the database and most of the
artifacts she'd been inputting didn't have any pictures
at all. Grabbing the camera and the keys and
clutching a few of the catalog sheets, the volunteer
climbed the steep steel stairs in the 1823 jail that led
to what was then the storage room.

Entering the room she saw that things were still a bit cluttered, but she was definitely making a dent. She glanced down at the pages in her hand. It was mostly clothing and all of it was reported to be in good condition. Why not photograph the pieces on the mannequins? She pulled a box down off the shelf and opened it. Between the layers of crisp, white tissue paper, everything looked in good shape, so she lifted out the first garment and draped it over the mannequin. That looked good, but as she stood back to take the picture she realized that the room around her subject was just too busy. There were boxes and frames, shelves and tables and what she needed was a nice blank white wall. The hall. That would work. There was plenty of space to work there. So, she carefully picked up the mannequin and placed it in the hall.

Taking photos of the clothing proved simple in this area and her task moved along swiftly. Reaching the last catalog page, the volunteer draped the final dress on the mannequin and stood back to make sure she could get the whole dress in the shot. Her left hand hung by her side as she focused the camera with her right. As she searched for the proper angle, someone reached out and gently touched her hand. Their thumb dragging across the back of her knuckles. Immediately, she looked around. How had someone managed to climb the stairs without her knowing?

But there was no one there. Her mind raced for answers. Perhaps a piece of tissue paper had grazed her hand as it fell from a nearby table. But no. The table was too far away and the tissue that this dress had been wrapped in was on the other side of the hall. She was certain she was alone, but equally certain that someone had just tried to say hello.

She was not the first one to have such a touching experience at the jail, nor do I suppose she will be the last. So don't be surprised if the next time you are in the jail, you feel more than a shiver down your spine.